TRAIN OF NOSTALGIA

TRAIN OF NOSTALGIA

A Collection of Poems and Paintings

Dr Christoday Raja Jayant Khess

KALPAZ

ISBN: 978-81-7835-996-0

Price: ₹ 360

First Published 2013

Published by

Kalpaz Publications
C-30, Satyawati Nagar,
Delhi - 110052
E-mail: kalpaz@hotmail.com Ph.: 9212142040

Laser Typesetting: Rajender Vashist, Delhi
Printed at: G. Print Process, Delhi

Cataloging in Publication Data--DK

Courtesy: D.K. Agencies (P) Ltd. <docinfo@dkagencies.com>

Khess, Christoday Raja Jayant.

Train of nostalgia : a collection of poems and paintings / Christoday Raja Jayant Khess.

p. cm.

Poems.

ISBN 9788178359960

1. Indic poetry (English). 2. Painting, Indic. I. Title.

DDC 823.92 23

Contents

Preface 9
Acknowledgements 11
List of Images 13
Childhood Days **19**
1. Train of Nostalgia 23
2. Kings of the Road 24
3. Boy's Toys 27
4. Separated 28
5. The Wayfinder Shoes 29
6. Firefighters 30
7. The Phantom 33
8. The Rooster Crows for You 34
9. Ode to the Beatles 37
10. The Hero 38
11. Royal in Its Ways 41
12. A Hero Betrayed 42
Observations **43**
13. Cheetah at Rest 44
14. Hypnotic Eyes 47
15. The Fall of Bengal 48
16. Judgement Day 49
17. Himalayas 50
18. Moved by the Railways 53
19. Digging up Graves 54
20. Holier than Thou 55
21. Uncanny Emotions 56

22. The Warrior and the King 57
23. The Adivasi 58
24. In Memory of a Goddess 61
25. A Celebration in Vain 62
26. Oh! Sons of the Soil 63
27. A Sad Realisation 64
28. A Personal View 65
29. The Crow 66
30. Pride of the Savannah 69
31. Some Thoughts 70
32. The Bogeyman 71
33. You Can't Run Away 72
Inspiring Notes 73
34. At the Borderline 74
35. The Beauty of Power 75
36. The Last of the Braves 76
37. Fall of a Mighty Sultan 79
38. The Man Who Rose from the Dust 80
39. A Tribute to Heroes of Kohima 81
40. I Dared 82
41. An Unsung Hero 85
42. Precious Moments 86
43. A Song of Patriotism 87
44. Don't Cry 88
45. Never Give Up 89
46. Cheer Up 90
47. Facts of Life 91
48. United They Stand 92
49. The Champion 95
50. Smoking Joe 96

Beautiful Moments 97
51. Haunted 98
52. Untamed Spirit 101
53. A Tribute to Things Beautiful 102
54. A Celebration of Beauty 105
55. Remembered 106
56. Kanaili—A Love Song 109
57. My Boy 110
In a Lighter Vein 111
58. Marked by Spots 112
59. Tale of Tail 115
60. Ode to Innocent Devils 116
61. Dancing in the Rain 117
62. Extinguish the Fire 118
63. Love in Distress 119
64. The Match 120
65. Holiwater 121
66. What, If 122
67. New Year's Blues 123
68. Those Who Love the Elderly 124
69. Not Cricket 125
70. When I am Eighty-Eight 126
71. Right or Wrong 127
72. Beware, the Vampire Loves You 128
73. The Snake Charmer 131
74. Difficult to Change 132
Love Songs 133
75. Girl 134
76. Fury of Love 135
77. The Dilemma 136

78. Honeymoon 139
79. The Unforgettable Moment 140
80. In Love 141
81. Silent Love 142
82. The Wait 143
83. Gentle Love 144
84. Anxious in Love 145
85. Reckless Abandon 146
86. Meek Surrender 147
87. Fruit of Love 148
In a Pensive Mood **149**
88. In Defence 150
89. Blinded 151
90. Between Life and Death 152
91. The Quest 153
92. Days of Despair 154
93. My Destiny and Me 155
94. It Weeps for Me 156
95. From the Heart 157
96. I Wonder 158
97. Beyond Death 159
98. A Thought from Within 160
99. India Divided 161
100. Farsightedness 162
101. Short of Greatness 163
102. Does It Stink? 164
103. The Crash 165
104. Creation 166
Epilogue **167**
105. Arrival of the Chill with Deepawali 168

Preface

TRAIN OF NOSTALGIA is a collection of poems and paintings which was conceived by me almost a decade ago. The paintings were supposed to facilitate the imagination associated with the printed words of the poems. However it was a difficult endeavour, hence it took a long time to complete this book. I would have liked to add more paintings but I was unable to accomplish this. Had it not been for the constant encouragement of my well wishers this work would have remained incomplete. I hope the readers enjoy this book which will take them through various phases of life as well as various emotional states.

Dr Christoday Raja Jayant Khess

Acknowledgements

My interest in English language can easily be traced back to my teachers, Fr. Rosner, Fr. Derickx and Mr Augustine Boroi, in high school. The Late Father Rosner in particular, instilled so much interest in us, both for prose and poetry, by his inimitable passionate style, that we have still not forgotten 'Julius Caesar' and 'Panorama' which he taught us in school. He was the person most responsible, for initiating a love for things in the printed form.

After my teachers there have been several special people, who have not only inspired me but also encouraged me to go ahead with this endeavour. I feel proud to acknowledge them, namely, Dr Mona Dhillon, Dr Jayati Simlai, Dr Paulina Khess and Dr P.K. Mukherjee. I would also like to acknowledge the interest shown by my son, Nikhil, in this project. I remember the awe in his eyes when I had read the 'Train of Nostalgia' to him. He was too young to understand most of what I had written then. Now he has grown up to be a fine young man.

I would like to give special thanks to Mr Nirmalya Chakraborty for his technical advice and help which was necessary to complete this work.

Dr Christoday Raja Jayant Khess

LIST OF IMAGES

1. Train of Nostalgia 17
2. Train of Nostalgia 21
3. Kings of the Road 25
4. Boy's Toys 26
5. Firefighters 31
6. The Phantom 32
7. The Rooster Crows for You 35
8. Ode to the Beatles 36
9. The Hero 39
10. Royal in its Ways 40
11. Cheetah at Rest 45
12. Hypnotic Eyes 46
13. Himalayas 51
14. Moved by the Railways 52
15. The Adivasi 59
16. In Memory of a Goddess 60
17. The Crow 67
18. Pride of the Savannah 68
19. The Beauty of Power 77
20. Last of the Braves 78
21. I Dared 83
22. An Unsung Hero 84
23. United They Stand 93
24. The Champion 94
25. Haunted 99

26. Untamed Spirit 100
27. A Tribute to Things Beautiful 103
28. A Celebration of Beauty 104
29. Remembered 107
30. Kanaili—A Love Song 108
31. Marked by Spots 113
32. Tale of Tail 114
33. Beware, the Vampire Loves You 129
34. The Snake Charmer 130
35. The Dilemma 137
36. Honeymoon 138

Train of Nostalgia

1. Train of Nostalgia

Childhood Days

2. Train of Nostalgia

TRAIN OF NOSTALGIA

Nothing filled my heart with passion,
Like a visit to a railway station,
To catch a glimpse of a locomotive engine;
Chugging into the platform, breathing fire,
Before it braked into a screeching halt,
Sending the crowd into pandemonium.

Hissing impatiently, while it had to wait,
For passengers to scurry inside the gate,
Before it could shriek in the countryside;
Puffing steam, to generate power,
Required to pull the bogies of iron,
To reach destinations at the right hour.

The savage beauties on the tracks,
Are reminiscent of those childhood days;
When the sight of advancing trains,
Captivated our young brains;
When these juggernauts in motion,
Inspired the children of this nation.

KINGS OF THE ROAD

Have you ever driven by night,
Blinded by glaring headlights,
Of mighty kings of the roads,
Approaching at a threatening speed.

These majestic beasts on the run,
Seldom need to blow their horns,
Because, of the sonorous groan,
Which makes their presence known.

Those who race against them,
Are unable to maintain the pace,
Because, they lack the stamina,
Which is the strength of these giants.

Traversing countless miles,
Both by day and night,
These trucks in flight,
Make a formidable sight.

When they move in a convoy,
Recklessly racing one another,
They worry about nothing at all,
Except, the sight of a police patrol.

3. Kings of the Road

4. Boy's Toys

BOY'S TOYS

When boys had time to dream,
The theme was invariably the same,
Driving an open Willys jeep,
Through slopes, precariously steep!

Had there been exchange-offers then,
They would have bartered their toys,
To possess those objects of joy,
And master the four by fours!

SEPARATED

Shining in their black shoes,
The young boisterous fools,
Hated to be kept in school,
Because, it was so full of rules.

The beautiful, silly girls,
Looking irresistible in their skirts,
Were attracted to these boys,
But, thought they made such a fuss.

Co-education was not yet in,
There were different schools then,
There was 'Xaviers', there was 'Loreto',
Separated by the fathers and nuns.

THE WAYFINDER SHOES

There was a time when young boys,
Wore the 'Wayfinders' to school,
The recommended boots by 'Bata'
King of the footwear industries,
Known for its ugly shoes.

Disappointing at first sight,
They turned into a source of delight,
When we discovered a compass inside,
And slipped them in our pockets,
To guide us everywhere.

In outdoor sessions,
Like classroom lessons,
When 'scouting' was in the curriculum,
We traced the course of fountains,
And scaled the peaks of mountains.

No matter wherever we were,
Shielded by these leather wears,
We were protected and secure,
So, even if we kicked at stones,
We did not break our bones.

We grew up wearing 'Wayfinders',
The rugged 'Bata' shoes,
To find direction in life,
And understand with time,
Endurance is required to triumph.

FIREFIGHTERS

Boys, all over the world,
Dream being firefighters;
Zipping along the streets,
In sleek firetenders.
Ringing a shrill bell;
As if to yell at them,
Who come in the way,
To block the road ahead.

Inducing a panic reaction,
In things, slow in motion;
As they race against time,
To reach a blazing site.
To douse the flames,
With jets of water;
Precariously perched on ladders,
Proving their steely characters.

5. Firefighters

6. The Phantom

THE PHANTOM

An enigma for the enemy,
Understood by the pygmy;
The ghost walked with devil,
A savage wolfish dog,
Committed to fight evil.

Mistaken for a bandit,
The hero of our times,
Dreaded by thugs in crime;
The hooded masked man,
Left a skull mark for a name.

THE ROOSTER CROWS FOR YOU

Before the sun steals the dew,
When it is still pleasant and cool,
And there is a freshness in the air;
The rooster crows for you,
To wake-up to enjoy the view.

So, hurry, get up soon,
Don't miss the beautiful dawn;
It will fill your heart with glee,
Which needs to spread every where,
To make the world a cheerful place.

7. The Rooster Crows for You

8. Ode to the Beatles

ODE TO THE BEATLES

Not long ago, after the great war,
In a small town Liverpool, in England,
Four boys were practicing to form a band,
That would take the world by storm.

The Beatles were preparing to hit the road,
Play incredible music like never before,
Inspire an entire generation to love,
Forget hatred and concentrate on rock.

John, Paul, George and Ringo,
Sang tunes, which became immortal,
The lyrics ignited the mind and soul,
Made youngsters all over to rock and roll.

THE HERO

My hero was unlike Hollywood stars,
Who portray illusions to win awards.
He was a legend called Robin Hood,
Who emerged from a faceless crowd.

The guardian angel of the oppressed
Was revered in poor neighbourhoods,
For his pledge to fight the greed
Of unscrupulous nobles, against all odds.

For the struggle against misdeeds,
A price was fixed for his head.
But, he met an end like rebels do,
An uncherised death by the woods.

9. The Hero

10. Royal in Its Ways

ROYAL IN ITS WAYS

The Royal Enfield of olden days,
Dominates the scene till today;
The way it conquers the curves,
It unsettles young nerves.

The beauty of man's dream,
Is this ageless mean machine;
Powered to ride on open fields,
It ignites the macho senses.

It sets the adrenaline surging,
Through the arteries and veins;
Astride on this vintage bike,
Everyone feels like a king.

A HERO BETRAYED

Fathered by the mighty sun,
But, abandoned by his own,
He grew up a commoner's son,
To become a generous man,
Who stood by his friends;
Yet, destiny conspired against him.

Deserted by cruel fate,
He met an unjust end;
But, he was the real winner,
Karan, the great hero,
Who gave away his life,
Because, he never refused to help.

Observations

CHEETAH AT REST

A poetry in motion,
Is a cheetah on the run,
But, at rest is no less,
Even for a moment.

Whether restricted by time,
To be frozen in a frame,
Or captured on a canvas,
By an artist's imagination.

A poetry in motion,
Is a cheetah on the run,
But, at rest is no less,
Even for a moment.

11. Cheetah at Rest

12. Hypnotic Eyes

HYPNOTIC EYES

Stealthily, he creeps towards the mark,
That has been identified in the dark-
Apparently, concealed by a camouflage,
Of the dark green foliage-
A deer, grazing grass.

Believing, to be hidden from the stripped coat,
That shines through the anxious moments,
Which spell doom for its kind,
As the tiger lives up to its fame-
The master of the game.

The royal cat of the Indian forests,
Has the hypnotic eyes,
Which paralyses the mind of the prey,
As it goes blank at the sight
Of this predator, at night.

THE FALL OF BENGAL

The traitors were exposed,
In the battlefield of Plassey,
When they let down their Nawab,
Sirajudowlla, grandson of the Khan.

The treachery of Mir Jaffar,
Led to his defeat in the war,
Won by East India Company,
Loyal to the British Crown.

The tyrants did not stop at that,
But, stabbed him to his death;
The ruins of Murshidabad,
Bear testimony to this tragic end.

Betrayed by the cowards,
Driven by lust for power,
Came the end of days of glory—
Fall of the Nizamut of Bengal.

JUDGEMENT DAY

In the palace of justice at Nuremberg,
The Nazis were put on trial,
By the victors of the war,
To answer for their crimes.

But, did anyone wonder then,
Who will sit on judgement,
On those who dropped the Atom bomb,
To sweep off millions from this world.

Will the end justify the means,
Adopted by winners of this cruel game,
Or, will things be reviewed again,
On 'Judgement Day' in heaven?

HIMALAYAS

Rising above the dense foliage,
Is the imposing Himalayan range,
Pride of new fold mountains,
Adorned with snow-capped peaks.

Abode of Gods and Goddesses;
Home to the mighty glaciers,
Source of the beautiful Ganges,
The holy river of this land.

Since days of ancient history,
It has stood in the way,
Unfazed by advancing armies,
To protect us from our enemies.

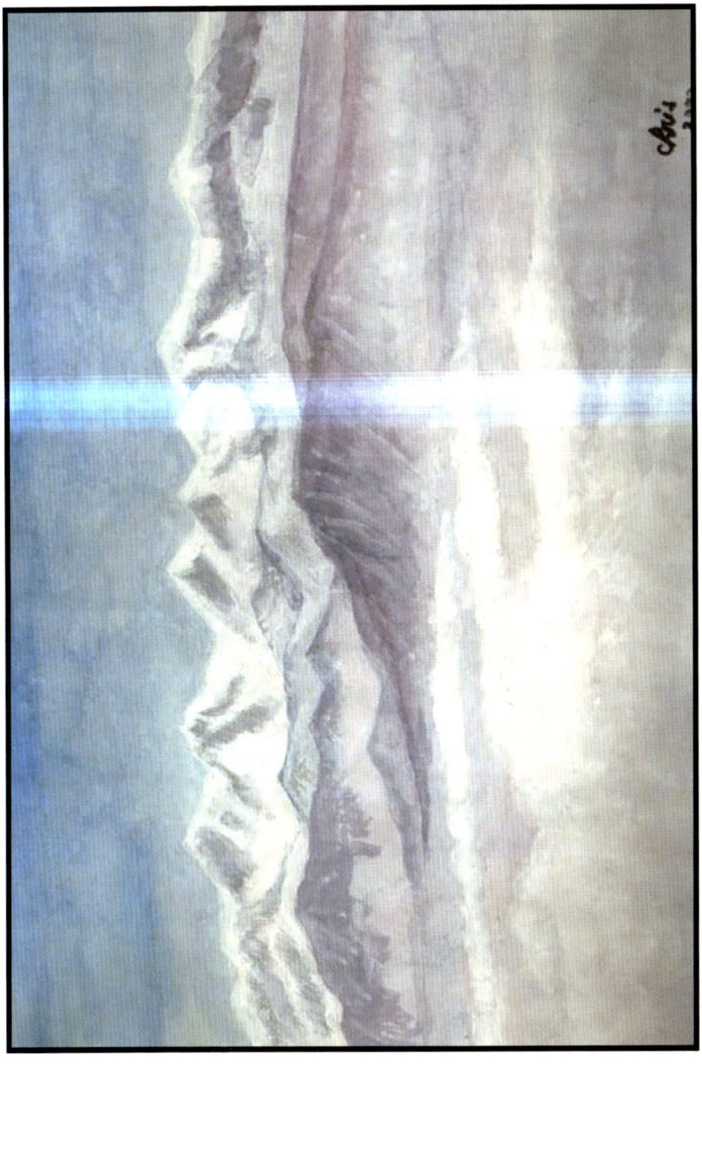

13. Himalayas

14. Moved by the Railways

MOVED BY THE RAILWAYS

This is a tribute to the railways,
The thing that moves in the country;
On the rails or off the tracks,
Seldom on time, frequently late.

Defamed by callous employees,
Not vigilant in their duties;
The target of terrorist attacks,
Which take away precious lives.

Yet, airways often fail to take-off,
Motorways are obstructed by road-blocks,
So, the train has to be the reliable one,
Which has to carry everyone.

DIGGING UP GRAVES

Pharaohs have been woken from their slumber,
So, should lesser mummies worry in sleep?
Whether, living mortals will dig up their graves,
To peep at them, for some silly reason,
Without realizing, such acts disturb the dead.

In the attempt to solve unknown mysteries,
Better left buried in the dust of history,
We dig out skeletons from their tombs,
Believing, the past will provide solutions,
To questions which do not have any answers.

In this quest to unearth the truth,
We get misled, like impressionable youths,
Who demolish mosques in search of temples,
Without understanding those sentiments,
Which are essential for human existence.

HOLIER THAN THOU

If you decide to renounce this world,
To go and meditate in a distant land,
With the hope to find peace of mind,
You have my blessing to go ahead;
May be you could discover in solitude,
What you did not find in this crowd.

Some would not agree with this attitude,
But, many more would not care,
Whether you do penance on a mountain,
Or hide yourself in a deep forest;
So, whatever you do in the end,
Please do not comeback as a saint!

UNCANNY EMOTIONS

The ocean stirs up strange emotions,
So, I am at sea by the shore;
The waves breaking into the beach,
Make me pensive deep within.

I begin to think of life on earth,
What it gives, what it takes;
Does it matter, whether we lose or win,
When the time comes to face our death.

The rise and fall of the tides,
Remind me of the beginning of end;
That which is created will be destroyed,
Dust will return to dust, and ashes to ashes.

THE WARRIOR AND THE KING

Birsa resisted the British Empire,
And fought them with a lot of ire;
But, it was not for our liberation,
As some of us like to declare.

'Jharkhand' was conceived by a man,
Who cared for his kith and kin;
But, no one gives credit to him,
For his farsighted vision and dream.

He was forsaken like a sinner,
By those blind to his contributions;
Which is visible to those who can see,
Like me and a few others as well.

Distinguished sons of this soil,
Both were above ordinary souls;
Yet, Birsa was a warrior,
While, Jaipal was the king.

THE ADIVASI

He was neither a Christian nor a Hindu,
Before the Aryans crossed river Sindhu,
To confuse his mind in a political game,
Make him doubt what he was, before they came;
Who will give him the sense to understand,
Ethnicity and religion are not the same.

Irrespective of his faith, he will belong to the pool
Of people, considered to be emotional fools;
Ruled by their hearts instead of the head,
Who shut their eyes and pretend to be blind;
Inspite of the conspiracy of the changing times,
He will remain an Adivasi, ignorant but kind.

15. The Adivasi

16. In Memory of a Goddess

IN MEMORY OF A GODDESS

Yesterday, they worshipped her like a Goddess,
When she looked radiant in the shinning lights;
A smile on the lips, benevolence in the eyes,
When everyone waited to be blessed by her sight.

Today, she is alone immersed in the deep,
Her beauty melting in the depths of the sea;
The memory of her magnificent presence,
Will soon fade away, without any trace.

A CELEBRATION IN VAIN

I saw them standing with their wares,
Concern wrought large on their face,
Whether they would earn their bread,
Or would they return empty hands;
I prayed, it would be different today.

Their infant 'state' had turned a toddler.
Which was expected to move forward,
But, had they measured the progress made,
They would have protested in rage,
Because, they saw not even a crawl.

For whom was this celebration meant?
Who, for generations had waited for change,
Could we rejoice when people were sad?
Without giving them a ray of hope—
Someday their future would be secure.

OH! SONS OF THE SOIL

Simple sons of the soil,
Who cannot change with time;
Even, if it rings the death knell,
And pushes you close to hell.

Who is going to help you,
If you cannot help yourselves?
Simple sons of the soil,
Oh! Sons of the soil!

A SAD REALISATION

When idols crumble down,
And legends fade into oblivion;
When heroes fall from grace,
And cease to impress the mind;
It leaves an emptiness behind,
Though we pretend not to care.

When distorted reflections,
Become visible in the light,
It invariably makes us sad;
This is a grim realization,
By a little innocent boy,
Who has grown to be a man.

A PERSONAL VIEW

A man called Marcel Proust has documented
The abilities of individuals of a special kind,
Who suffer to bestow their gifts on this world,
Often becoming subjects to ridicule and scorn,
For eventhough they appear completely sane,
They are capable of acts which are insane.

Could they be the so-called 'neurotics',
Who are known to swim against the tide,
Not acknowledged today by diagnostic manuals,
Their existence is recorded in psychiatric annals,
When the world was mesmerized by their malady,
Till Freud analyzed the human psyche.

This view is based on personal thoughts,
Which could be nowhere near the truth,
So, do not make it a basis for controversy,
Which would pitch me against my colleagues,
Because, I state what I genuinely feel,
Without the fear of stirring a hornet's nest.

THE CROW

The bird that no one adores,
Is an avis that no one knows;
A dark angel, called a crow,
Who greets us in the morn,
Perched on a treetop at the door.

One who scavenges for our health,
Could have been the best in black;
But, the cuckoo took this place,
Because, she brought it to this world,
By hatching it out of the egg.

17. The Crow

18. Pride of the Savannah

PRIDE OF THE SAVANNAH

The pride of the savannah grassland,
Are the masai and the lion;
They belong to a proud legacy,
Which is as old as mankind,
When man and beast lived side by side.

Though a bit wary of each other,
Yet, in awe of the other's power,
Which can destroy the other;
The pride of the savannah grassland,
Are the masai and the lion.

SOME THOUGHTS

Tsunamis wreck havoc on the shore,
Tempests raise waves from the floor,
Deserts stir up a storm out of dust,
Oceans quench no one's thirst.

Crowds induce feeling of emptiness,
Yearning arouses anguish that pains,
A twitch in heart, causes a flutter in mind,
Such things happen all the time.

THE BOGEYMAN

He teases his gut with countless pegs,
Burns his lungs with never ending puffs,
Clouds his mind with uninspiring thoughts,
Which make him hopeless from within.

He was bright and cheerful once,
When the heart was strong and young,
Then he had lots and lots of fun,
But, today he is the bogeyman of town.

YOU CAN'T RUN AWAY

You can run away from everyone,
But, you can't run away from self;
It will cling to you like a shadow,
Till you go inside the grave.

You can run away from people,
But, you can't run away from life;
Till death will permit you,
The liberation from this world.

Inspiring Notes

AT THE BORDERLINE

Feeling lonely deep inside,
Bored with things by her side;
She struggles to control impulses,
Which threaten to destroy her existence;
Yet, she is a darling sweetie-pie,
Sensitive from the core of her heart.

She is torn in opposite directions,
By the desires and duties of life;
Caught between the devil and deep sea,
Her options are limited indeed;
This makes her depressed at times,
As she feels split into conflicting halves.

THE BEAUTY OF POWER

For countless artists,
The subject of a portrait,
Is a locomotive engine,
Not a pretty mademoiselle.

I wonder, why this attraction,
Is it a mere fascination,
Or is it sheer passion,
Not for beauty, but power?

Can anyone answer this question,
Better than George Stephenson,
Who invented these machines,
That led to a revolution!

THE LAST OF THE BRAVES

Adorned with beautiful feathers,
Bare-bodied on the back of a stallion,
The last of the braves, sits straight;
Unfazed by the massacre around,
He is prepared to kill for the land,
Which belongs to his forefathers.

Once, an undiscovered world,
Unknown to the white man,
Is on the verge of destruction;
Soon, the bisons in the open fields,
The Red Indians on their steeds,
Will be things from the past.

The bronze figure with a tomahawk,
Has a daunting task ahead,
To silence the guns loaded to fire;
Inspite of the odds against him,
He will not back down to the enemy,
But, fight till the tragic end.

19. The Beauty of Power

20. Last of the Braves

FALL OF A MIGHTY SULTAN

The Cauvery flowed in turbulence,
While the enemy besieged the fort,
To capture an indomitable tiger-
The mighty sultan of Mysore.

The distinguished son of a warrior,
Was a valiant soldier,
Who lived by his sword,
To win several battles,
A reason for concern for the foe.

But, betrayed by treacherous times,
He caught a bullet between the eyes,
To fall from the back of his horse,
Into a sea of the dead.

Yet, the heavens were pleased,
He fell in a battlefield,
Clad in shining armour,
Soaked in the blood of valour,
To die a death of honour.

THE MAN WHO ROSE FROM THE DUST

This is the story of an extraordinary man,
Born in the wilderness of this forestland,
Without advantages of the privileged ones,
He looked like an ordinary son.

He laboured to master his lessons,
Burning the kerosene lamp,
To remove the darkness of night,
Which would engulf the rest of his kind.

He was a man who rose from the dust,
To change his destiny with hard work,
And not leave it at the mercy of luck,
Like those who believe in shortcuts.

A TRIBUTE TO HEROES OF KOHIMA

A gift by the Angami chiefs,
To the people of the East,
Kohima city, by the Jafu peak,
Is the pride of the Naga Hills.

Witness to a cruel war,
Between the Brits and Japs,
When braves fell like ninepins,
To save unknown lives.

They sacrificed their today,
For an uncertain tomorrow,
To secure our future in time,
Shedding their precious blood.

Spare a thought, when alone,
For those who fell by a tennis court,
Make amends, before it is late,
And pay tribute to those heroes.

I DARED

I dared to chase my dream,
Through the darkness of night,
To the brightness of daylight;
Something, few could do.

Even if life was a nightmare,
From which there was escape;
They were unable to get away,
Because, they were afraid.

Haven't you ever wondered,
Had they been brave enough,
To risk everything they had;
They could have become kings.

21. I Dared

22. An Unsung Hero

AN UNSUNG HERO

To feel the breeze whistling by,
He wanted to fly in the sky,
Soar above the distant clouds,
To see the earth below,
Like mighty eagles do.

But alone in this flight,
He was engulfed by ailments,
So, he plunged into an abyss,
Which immersed him in darkness,
This obscured his view.

He aspired to conquer the skies,
Like most heroes would,
So, what if he did not succeed,
He did give it a try,
This his friend knows.

PRECIOUS MOMENTS

Life is a chain of precious moments,
Which pass us by, before we realize;
Time will flow, even if we cease to grow;
Or be left behind, to stagnate alone.

Let us walk, even if the pace is slow,
And not languish in the past;
To live in the present, without worries,
That distract us from our task.

Let us endure pain to earn pleasure,
And experience heaven on earth;
Because, if rebirth is not certain,
This could be our only chance.

A SONG OF PATRIOTISM

I begin this song of patriotism with a borrowed line—
'Rise all ye countrymen, stand up for your pride.'
Do not pretend to sleep with eyes opened wide,
Because, the mirror will reflect the shame, we cannot hide,
Till, like grains of sand, we are swept with every tide.

Five decades after independence we are not liberated,
As people of this country still feel threatened.
Isn't it time, to stop those who spread hatred,
Time to join hands instead of feeling scared,
And speak our minds without being intimidated.

It does not require arms to start a revolution,
Nor does it require bloodshed for human salvation.
Just a simple thought is enough for the inspiration,
Which need not be a product of profound wisdom.
So, will you stand united to save our beloved nation?

DON'T CRY

Don't cry my little child,
Because, it is useless to cry.
Leave your sadness behind,
And start looking ahead,
Soon your tears will dry.

Your vision will become clear,
As you will come to realize,
People who never give up to try,
Even in situations of 'do or die',
Have learnt not to cry.

NEVER GIVE UP

God had barely rested after Creation,
When the Devil conquered man,
As he led Adam and Eve to temptation;
The Almighty seeing them fall from grace,
Did not condemn them to hell,
To suffer forever in pain.

So, when your efforts are sabotaged by evil brains,
Do not throw up your hands in despair,
But, pull yourself up again,
To forgive your detractors and carry on,
Because, it will make you strong,
Never to let yourself down.

CHEER UP

Whenever you are upset and feel blue,
Don't you become oblivious of the view,
Which needs to be appreciated by you,
You see nothing, as you stare through,
As if everything were untrue.

Don't you miss the budding flowers,
That blossom in the monsoon showers,
To cover the land with a rainbow of colours,
Which you are unable to notice in sadness,
As heavens weep to give you happiness.

FACTS OF LIFE

Some facts are shrouded in mystery,
But, simple truths are there to be seen,
Like, blazing summers end with rains,
When, the land is drenched by showers,
To quench the thirst with water.

When clouds are replaced by sunshine,
Then, roses grow over prickly thorns,
And love blossoms inspite of hate,
To teach us the value of life—
Which cannot be secured by strife.

UNITED THEY STAND

Watched by evil eyes,
Which pierce the darkness;
These mammoths look insecure,
As they wait for time to pass.

Huddled close to each other,
In the loneliness of the forest;
United they will stand tall,
Divided they will fall.

23. United They Stand

24. The Champion

THE CHAMPION

The champion has fallen to the ground,
Age caught up, so a youngster has won;
The first time things appear upside down,
Bones are intact, but the heart is broken,
The fists are sore, the mind is clouded.

He is the man who stood in the middle,
Exchanging blows round after round,
To earn with pride every single pound;
He has just lost a title, not his honour,
He is a champion, he should be proud.

SMOKING JOE

A poor young boy left home behind
To come to Philadelphia to earn a name;
The five foot eleven and a half overweight soul,
Was determined to become a heavy weight champ.

To earn the gold medal in the Olympic ring
He would have to fight with a broken finger,
The odds were against him, yet he would win;
Which he did, after knocking his opponent to the floor.

Then came the cataract which dimmed his vision,
Yet, he did not get overwhelmed by the situation;
He entered the arena against men who were formidable,
Who outweighed and dwarfed him by their size.

Smoking Joe always came charging at them,
Head first followed by the heart of a man,
Who could not be stopped by jabbering or jabs,
Relentlessly he would push forward, evading the blows.

He never pushed anyone back at the ropes,
He never held anyone into a clinch;
He kept coming in, smothering punches thrown at him,
He was a simple Joe, who should have been the king.

Beautiful Moments

HAUNTED

I have been preoccupied till now,
By a face I was unable to see,
Because, she had her back to me;
Drying her hair in the sunshine,
In front of a tumbling cascade,
Oblivious of this curious world;
She will be remembered,
As the unknown maid,
Who will haunt me till the end.

25. Haunted

26. Untamed Spirit

UNTAMED SPIRIT

She is the unbridled filly,
That gallops with the wind;
The untamed spirit,
Born to roam free.

She is the mighty wave,
That cannot be held at bay.
She crashes against rocks
That stand in her way.

She is the dream,
Of men who are tired
From the rigours of life,
Which take away their time.

A TRIBUTE TO THINGS BEAUTIFUL

By the side of a sea, in the dusty sands,
Stands tall, man's devotion to God,
Beautifully carved out of sand stone,
But, forsaken by Him, it lies alone.

There, amidst those lofty ruins,
I saw perfection, flawed just by a stitch;
A face marked by a beauty spot,
Like the moon, which looks perfect with dots.

Man's endeavours may go futile,
But, things blessed shall never die;
Poetries inscribed on rocks may fade,
But, things etched in the mind shall stay.

27. A Tribute to Things Beautiful

28. A Celebration of Beauty

A CELEBRATION OF BEAUTY

The fading light in the distant sky,
Was disappearing into the night;
Illuminating things on its way,
Before it became dark.

The evening breeze was gathering speed,
When I spotted two beautiful maids.
The glimpse of them is still so fresh,
Imprinted deep in my mind.

Draped in sarees, flaming red,
Coloured by the shade of a setting sun;
They reminded me of Durga and Kali,
So dazzling was their radiance.

As the wind blew against the tress,
To expose their naked face;
They blushed in front of my eyes,
Which were captivated by their sight.

Much later, I realized a fact,
Beauty cannot be overshadowed,
By those who paint themselves,
To hide the lines of age.

REMEMBERED

How many might have toiled,
In the scorching heat of day,
To pile the stones, block by block,
Till a masterpiece was created,
In the dry sands of Egypt,
By the mighty river Nile.

Their labour was not in vain,
Because, people remember them,
Whenever they see the ruins,
Still so magnificent,
Thousands of years later,
It touches the heart and soul.

The Pharaohs and the slaves,
Who matched skills with brains,
To chisel the rocks to shape,
And leave behind the wonders,
That can be counted on fingertips,
Will never be forgotten by man.

29. Remembered

30. Kanaili—A Love Song

KANAILI—A LOVE SONG

Do not be swayed by your fervent emotions,
Kanaili, do not cross the river for heavens' sake,
The turbulent stream is sweeping things away,
As the water is swirling, rising and falling.

The monsoon is in a fury, pouring rain,
It will drown anyone who is reckless or insane,
Kanaili, do not cross the river for heavens' sake,
Soon I will be there by your side again

MY BOY

I remember your innocent face,
Wrinkled like an old man,
But, unmarked by lines of age;
You had not opened your eyes for me,
To search my reflection in you.

Then you had slept like a darling,
From the morning till evening,
While I had waited impatiently,
So that I could be seen by you,
To be recognized in your dreams.

In a Lighter Vein

MARKED BY SPOTS

For fear of being exposed,
In the middle of the night,
While perched on a treetop,
Somewhere deep in a forest,
The leopard wears a coat.
Marked all over by blots,
That look like black dots,
Which cannot be washed off,
Yet, he is happy with the spots.

31. Marked by Spots

32. Tale of Tail

TALE OF TAIL

This tale of the tail
Is not a fairytale,
But, the story of an angel
Who fell from grace;
He shed his wings of feather
To grow a tail instead,
Which became so long,
It reached all corners,
To play on people's mind.

His face was covered
By a Halloween mask,
To frighten away monsters
By the devilish looks;
Capped by pointed horns,
Sharper than ordinary thorns,
Which could pierce through
The defense of conscience,
And steal away the soul.

ODE TO INNOCENT DEVILS

Behind the innocent eyes
Of a young child,
Could there be a devil's mind?
I have asked this question before,
Though it sounds weird.

Yet, haven't you had doubts
About these little angels,
When they play the fool
In front of those teachers,
Who lack a sense of humour.

When you get the dreaded call
To be in school before the bell;
Doesn't it make you feel unwell
To think you have to go through hell,
And still keep you cool!

DANCING IN THE RAIN

They sway in the humid air;
Two kings dancing in the rain;
Twirling and twisting,
Entwined like creepers,
Two kings dancing in the rain.
The intent is not sinister,
The fangs are not lethal;
There is only love in the mind,
While these cobras dance in the rain.

EXTINGUISH THE FIRE

Love ignites a flame within,
Which cannot be doused by water,
But, only extinguished by tears;
So, shed the streams of emotion,
Before your heart burns,
And turns into a heap of ash;
Get hold of yourself,
And spurn your admirer,
Before he sparks a fire.

LOVE IN DISTRESS

The woman is the mistress,
Who puts a noose around her master,
To leash him by the neck thereafter,
And chain him down forever.

He is domesticated into a pet,
Who wags his tail at the drop of a hat,
To get the approval of his soulmate,
Who becomes indifferent like a cat.

THE MATCH

He is a serene ocean,
Appearing calm and quiet;
But, if you throw a pebble,
He will break into ripples.

She is a wild Amazon,
Rushing in a mighty cascade;
Don't try to block her,
For, you will be washed away.

He is a solid mountain,
Appearing firm and strong;
But, if you blast him,
He will be shattered to pieces.

She is an active volcano,
With molten lava within;
Don't let her erupt,
For, you will be burnt to ashes.

HOLIWATER

Once I was caught in a crossfire,
In a place across the holy river;
Where people were splashing each other,
With anything soluble in water.

Sticky mud and cowdung cakes,
Were aimed at beautiful cheeks;
To turn them red with anger,
When Holi was played without colours.

WHAT, IF

If Eve had not held Adam's hand,
And led him to civilisation;
Would he have got lost alone,
In the naked wilderness of Eden?

If Helen did not have the face,
To launch a thousand ships;
Would the Iliad have been written,
To celebrate the Trojan war?

If Shahjahan had perished,
And Mumtaz had lived;
Would she have built Taj Mahal,
In memory of their love?

If people had not become heart broken,
After hopelessly falling in love;
Would they have scribbled nonsense,
And believed them to be poems?

NEW YEAR'S BLUES

How will you usher in the New Year,
With a smile or tears in the eyes?
Will you look forward or look back in gloom,
Make resolutions to break them by noon?

Will you be drowning your sorrow alone,
Or sharing loneliness with an unknown fellow?
Will you be dancing with someone's dame,
Or spending quiet moments with your ma'am?

Whichever way you welcome the New Year,
Whether in a happy or in a sad mood;
The rest of the year will be still ahead,
So, do not end up with a heavy head.

THOSE WHO LOVE THE ELDERLY

Girls who fall for men, who are old and lazy,
Soon realize, they do not become crazy,
Like heroines of Mills and Boon stories;
When they discover, old men are such a bore,
Who disturb them at night because they snore,
Then their notion of an experienced heartthrob,
Is shattered like a mirror, which falls on the floor.

Falling for the elderly is next to madness,
And for saying this, I beg forgiveness,
From young ladies who need to grow,
And learn about things they should ignore;
Like males, who are more than forty-four,
Who should better be left alone;
After this, need I say anything more?

NOT CRICKET

In the desert kingdom of Sharjah,
A sport was introduced by a Sheikh,
Which was played by eleven,
Thoroughbred gentlemen, all of them,
Donned in colourful gears,
Who, unfortunately, fought a war,
With men in another colour.

This game involving a bat and ball,
Caused so much agony and pain,
In the nations of the losing teams,
That it had to be abandoned soon,
Amidst allegations of unfair play,
That money exchanged hands,
Giving cricket a bad name.

WHEN I AM EIGHTY-EIGHT

When I am around eighty eight,
And my brain is knotted up in tangles,
With plaques declaring me senile,
I will stop worrying about things
Like, names of presidents, past and present.

I will only remember, not to forget
To hide my old name plate,
Even if I am mistaken for Alzheimer;
I would not like to be disturbed in sleep,
While I see my favourite dreams.

RIGHT OR WRONG

Some live for the future,
So, they save and store,
For an uncertain tomorrow;
While, some beg and borrow,
What they need for the moment,
To enjoy the pleasures around;
Who is right and who is wrong?
Don't ask me this, for now,
Because, I haven't found it out!

BEWARE, THE VAMPIRE LOVES YOU

Beware of the dark cloak,
Which looks sinister like hell,
Because, it covers the evil,
Which bears the name Draculla;
Beware, the vampire loves you!

Beware of the sharp fangs,
Which are eager to dig into you,
To suck you till your blood is dry,
And you are no more than a corpse;
Beware, the vampire loves you!

33. Beware, the Vampire Loves You

34. The Snake Charmer

THE SNAKE CHARMER

Mesmerised by the music,
Played through a flute;
She was swayed by his charm,
To end up in his arms.

So captivating were his moves,
She remained clinging to his neck;
This snake charming man,
Could have his way with snakes.

DIFFICULT TO CHANGE

Those who are sceptical about things,
Like a toad becoming a prince,
Will understand these lines,
Which I pen down for them,
Somethings will remain the same,
Some habits are difficult to change,
Like passion for life, and craving for wine.

Love Songs

GIRL

A girl who became famous,
Did not keep her feet together;
She spread them far apart,
To gain a wider access.

She traversed up and down,
To discover unknown secrets;
By the end, she became tired,
But, earned a lot of admirers.

FURY OF LOVE

She carefully combs her hair,
After settling the folds,
In front of a dressing table,
Which has an adoring mirror,
Impressed by her figure.

Preparing to overwhelm someone,
Who is unaware of her existence;
She will use her feminine grace,
Concealed in a revealing dress,
To attract his attention towards her.

She will pursue him with patience,
Till he becomes aware of her;
Then snub him for satisfaction,
Because, though she is in love,
She is scorned by his ignorance.

THE DILEMMA

Emily, in love, in the land of gold,
With a cowboy, who walked tall;
Worried as time slipped out of hand,
Would her yearning ever end?

Whenever she saw him riding into the sunset,
She searched for tears, dried by the wild west;
Then, she would wonder whether to wait,
Or cross over to greener pastures ahead!

Emily, in love, in the land of gold,
With a cowboy, who walked tall;
Worried as time slipped out of hand,
Would her yearning ever end?

35. The Dilemma

36. Honeymoon

HONEYMOON

She waits alone in apprehension,
To hear the creak of the door,
Which shall indicate to her,
The arrival of the groom.

She crosses her arms over the breasts.
And squeezes her legs together,
As she trembles in the humid air,
Like a weightless feather.

A clock chimes in the darkness,
Reminding her of the approaching time,
Which will change her life forever,
After which, she will be a virgin no more.

THE UNFORGETTABLE MOMENT

Radiant under a glowing moon,
You looked a fairy queen;
The ethereal beauty of the skies,
Reflected in your bright eyes.

Spellbound, I stared at you,
That night in the wilderness;
My heart, full of tender feelings,
In a special moment, in the darkness.

IN LOVE

A gentle breeze caresses her skin,
While it glows under the moon;
The silky hair scattered everywhere,
Is entangled in knots by the air.

Her tender face is flushed with passion,
As emotions stirrup deep within;
It spreads warmth to every pore,
To ignite the flame of love.

SILENT LOVE

They are in love with each other,
So, they share silence together,
Lest the voice croaks or tears roll.

When they are upset and lonely,
They exchange emotions silently,
Lest they end up saying too much.

They have learnt from each other,
When to speak, when to be quiet,
When to express love in silence.

THE WAIT

My darling squats by the Ganges,
Immersed in the music of ragas;
Experiencing celestial moments,
While, far away I sit by myself;
Counting seconds, which will herald the day,
When she will be in my arms again!

GENTLE LOVE

My love for you is tender,
Too inconspicuous for you to see;
It may not pierce you like a dart,
So that your heart bleeds for me.

My love is a gentle breeze,
Not strong to sweep you off your feet;
It will caress your silky skin,
But, may not send you into a spin.

My love is guided by reason,
Which may fall short of passion;
So, every time you spot my potbelly,
Your legs may not turn to jelly.

ANXIOUS IN LOVE

Someday he will proclaim his love,
Which he has planned for long,
But, whenever he approaches her door,
His heart goes out of control,
And it starts galloping like a colt.

Even before he can utter a word,
He begins to gasp for fresh air,
As he trembles like a leaf,
When he runs out of breath,
And his limbs turn cold.

RECKLESS ABANDON

Her bosoms heave beneath the sheet,
While perspiration drips from the head,
As she sways in reckless abandon,
Coming to grips with the situation.

The dynamite inside the tunnel,
Will explode into a heightened awareness;
Lights will be heard, sounds will be seen,
As she will reach the peak of ecstasy.

MEEK SURRENDER

She wraps around her lover,
Breathing down his neck;
Hypnotized by her passion,
He is frozen into a statue,
Stiff like a ramrod,
Knocked off his senses.

She tests his mettle,
Without giving him a chance,
To try to gain control,
Over things slipping out of hand,
Leading to a meek surrender,
Before her enticing ways.

FRUIT OF LOVE

She writhes in pain on the floor,
To deliver the joy of life,
A reminder of the love,
When two hearts became one,
In a moment of passion,
When the seed of desire,
Was implanted in her womb,
To grow with time inside,
And become the fruit,
Which is reaped in labour.

In a Pensive Mood

IN DEFENCE

The men who walk the streets,
Are unlike me, I know;
Because, I do not fit the norms,
Laid for the abnormally sane.

The dark side of the mind,
The hidden self inside;
Tells me, I can not be damned,
Because, at times I behave insane.

BLINDED

In my strife with conflicts in life,
I seldom saw things in the proper light,
Because, I was plagued with illusions,
Which made my vision unclear.

This fascination for the unreal,
Blinded me to such an extent,
I kept seeing things which did not exist,
Like mirages in the desert sand.

Castles I built, were blown to dust.
Shadows I chased, disappeared in dusk.
Now, I yearn to find my insight,
And leave these memories behind.

BETWEEN LIFE AND DEATH

Do you realize, the two best days of our life,
Are the day we are born and the day we die,
When everyone that matters is by our side,
Even if they are not there in our hour of need;
When we struggle alone to make ends meet,
Performing Herculean tasks to earn our bread,
Slowly killing ourselves in an attempt to live!

We are unable to appreciate a simple fact,
More so, when we lie helplessly on the bed,
Because of the peculiar state of our mind-
Which at birth, is as good as dead,
And at death, is no more there—
That people are playing their part in an act,
Which begins with life and ends with death.

THE QUEST

I went back into the past
To a bygone era,
In search of happiness
Which eludes me till now,
But, all I found were ruins
Of things magnificent once.

I dared into the future too,
Looking for the castles
Built in my dreams,
But, I found heaps of rubble,
Bricks, stones and concrete,
Waiting to be cleared up.

Now, I am rooted to the ground,
Trying to find my bearings around;
Taking stock of the situation,
As it is at this moment;
Still hoping to find happiness,
If it is somewhere to be found!

DAYS OF DESPAIR

Once I had seen a full moon,
On a night filled with gloom.
Now, I grope in the darkness,
As I yearn for a source of brightness.

Before, I got lost in the wilderness,
I had sighted the path to heaven;
But, time has passed so soon,
It seems like a distant dream.

In this world, happiness is a boon,
So, I brood alone in my room,
Whether, I will see the moon again,
Before, I meet my doom?

MY DESTINY AND ME

How long will I believe in forecasts,
Based on silly horoscopes,
Determined by stars and planets,
That are beyond my control?

How long will I blame things on destiny,
Which go out of my hand,
When I act, without a thought,
For consequences, I cannot stand?

IT WEEPS FOR ME

When the mind is tormented,
And the heart full of woe;
There is no way for me to show,
My anguish and sorrow.

The voice invariably fails,
When I yearn to express myself;
Words desert me then,
When I need them the most.

Today the tears have dried,
Emotions do not reach the eyes;
Hence, my pen weeps for me,
With these lines, instead!

FROM THE HEART

Today, I feel drained and fatigued,
As, life's complexities intrigue my mind;
While, I am overwhelmed by my heart's desire,
I am scared of being destroyed by hell's fire.

I have come to realize, God is great indeed,
He not only gave us a heart, but also a mind;
Don't mistake this poem for a tale of sorrow,
I believe there will be a brighter tomorrow.

I WONDER

Sometimes, I wonder
When I am alone,
And feel a bit forlorn;
Who will remember me,
After I am gone,
When I will turn to dust,
Inside a dark hole;
Identified as a tomb,
Which will bear my name,
Engraved on a stone.

BEYOND DEATH

Someday, when I will lie in a casket,
With folded hands on my chest,
Will I expect everyone to be there,
To bid me the last farewell,
And walk with me till my grave,
With candles, joss-sticks and flowers,
To mark the place, where I will rest forever,
Left in peace by all the gentry,
To live in your mind thereafter,
An immortal life, beyond my death.

A THOUGHT FROM WITHIN

As I pen down these emotions,
Which flow from deep within,
I wonder, if it has been expressed before;
Yet, I do not want to hold them back,
But, want to share them with all,
In the belief, I might have a point to make;
Even though, it may not be worth a quote.
For intelligent people to take note.

If life were full of happiness and bliss,
Everything were perfect, with nothing amiss,
With nothing to pray for or wish;
Wouldn't it have appeared meaningless,
Whether we were existing at all;
So, to stop us from getting bored of living,
To make us appreciate we are still breathing,
God gave us a bit of pain and suffering!

INDIA DIVIDED

Hind, the plains beyond river Sindh,
Is headed towards destruction,
Shrouded in a cloud of ignorance,
Cradle of civilization, almost in ruins.

Land of agriculture, refined by culture,
Proud of a glorious past,
Once, a jewel in the crown,
Is broken into segments today.

To be an Indian now,
The caste has to be verified first,
Then a quota has to be assigned,
For an identity till the end.

FARSIGHTEDNESS

There was a time not long ago
When nothing bothered me at all,
Whether I saw a monster
Or heard the devil talk,
Till I went to a graveyard,
The day I had nothing to do.

That night I lay awake
Trying to comprehend,
The farsightedness of the man,
Who planned ahead of death,
And booked a piece of land,
To rest there after the end.

SHORT OF GREATNESS

He will be missed by some,
But, will be mourned by none;
Because, his quest for excellence,
Was cursed by everyone.

A life devoid of happiness,
Ceased with his last breath;
A wretched death for a man,
Who fell short of greatness.

DOES IT STINK?

The blood that flows in his veins,
Is not blue, but is red;
It leaves a stain behind,
Whenever he happens to bleed.

Does it have a primeval stink,
Common to things primitive,
That managed to survive with time,
To become stale like wine?

THE CRASH

He falls from perilous heights
Which he reaches in his frenzied flights,
When the mind is reckless sans insight
And the heart is ecstatic without fright.

He plunges into the depths of despair
And contemplates to end a life full of sorrow;
His vision is blurred with tears of sadness
So, all he can see are clouds of darkness.

CREATION

God planned this planet with a purpose,
So, he made the world beautiful for us,
By creating the seas and mountains,
Which is told in the book of Genesis.

Let us protect our earth, animals and trees,
Which were made to give us happiness;
Or else this poet will sit and wonder,
By creating man, did God do a blunder.

Epilogue

ARRIVAL OF THE CHILL WITH DEEPAWALI

My mother-in-law came calling
On a dark Deepawali evening,
Her path lighted by earthen lamps
Because the moon had hidden in shame;

Everything seemed frozen and still
As she sat upright and straight
Staring at the empty ceiling,
Without any warm feelings;

The room was full of empty stares
As the furrowed lines of divide
Etched deep in the forehead
Prevented contact of the eyes;

Shifting gaze and fidgety legs
Muffled the sound of the ticking clock,
Yet, dinner was served on time
As crackers ushered the chilling days ahead.